PAUSE

Also by Joan McIver Gibson

A Field Guide to Good Decisions: Values in Action

PAUSE

HOW TO TURN TOUGH CHOICES INTO STRONG DECISIONS

Joan M Gibson

JOAN MCIVER GIBSON, PH.D.

Copyright © 2013 by Joan McIver Gibson, Ph.D.

All rights reserved. No portion of this book may be reproduced, by any process or technique, without the express written consent of the publisher, except in the case of brief quotations embodied in critical reviews and certain other noncommercial uses permitted by copyright law.

Published by Joan McIver Gibson, Ph.D.

Albuquerque, New Mexico, United States of America

Ordering information at joanmgibson.com

ISBN 978-0-615-65313-6 (paperback)

Library of Congress Control Number: 2013901867

Book and cover design: Jennifer Pontzer, Concept Green LLC

Photographs: Ann Zelle © 2012

10 9 8 7 6 5 4 3 2 1

For Robin

RECOMMENDATION FOR *PAUSE*

We all face difficult decisions when confronted by troubling family situations or by events that demand attention given our leadership role in a community or corporate enterprise. Joan McIver Gibson gives us a roadmap to help each of us slow down, define the issue and use our deep-set values to anchor a decision framework.

All of us have experienced "no perfect answer without downsides." Joan points out that almost every difficult decision presents a choice between competing and often mutually exclusive fundamental values. What are we to do? *Pause* should be our first response: Use the guidelines to better decision making. These guidelines (included in a Decision-Making Worksheet) make the choice to take action possible and effective.

In the process of evaluating the situation and reflecting on our own strongest values, we can begin to build honest explanation points to communicate our decisions to others who are impacted by our choices. We all look for an answer that will be the best resolution and be understood, and hopefully accepted, by those we love or lead; *Pause* will help us get there.

Mary Graham Davis
President, Davis Consulting Group
Chair of the Board, Mount Holyoke College

CONTENTS

Foreword — xi
Introduction — xiii

SEEING
Where Am I? — 5
Where Are You? — 9
What Matters? — 13

BELIEVING
What Matters Most? — 21
Why? — 25
Must It Hurt? — 29

DOING
What Are My Choices? — 37
What Fits? — 41
What Do I Say? — 45

FINAL THOUGHTS
Conclusion — 55
Worksheets — 57
Acknowledgements — 61
Sources for Quotations — 63
About the Author — 65
Note from the Designer — 67

FOREWORD

Three summers ago, over a span of roiling weeks, I faced the toughest decision of my life.

Or so I believed at the time.

I gleaned information from writers I respect in *The New York Times* and from on-line sources; I spoke privately to professionals in the health field and received opinions to support all sides of a mounting family crisis. Finally, on my own, numb with concern and running out of time to forge a plan, I took a long, deep breath and did the best I could with the evidence at hand.

The result was far from perfect, but it was a start.

Had I had this spirited resource book by Joan McIver Gibson, I might have saved hours of flailing, felt less isolated in reaching a course of action and, ultimately, realized that tougher decisions would no doubt lie ahead, but that each could be addressed with fresh insights and a modicum of new confidence.

In *Pause: How to Turn Tough Choices into Strong Decisions*, Dr. Gibson presents real cases that can apply to many of life's stumbling blocks. With clarity and compassion, she shows that our thorniest challenges do not involve differentiating between the forces of good and evil, as in comic books, but between the merits of good and good, or good and slightly better.

Part of the struggle in decision making is to resist writing all the parts, speaking all the roles, presuming to know others' reactions and, therefore, failing to ask and to listen. This can lead to the discomforting limbo of avoiding an issue for fear of conflict, or wallowing too long in the energy-zapping slough of "Why me?"

What a conceit. Why any of us?

In chapter after chapter, Joan Gibson's curiosity about the potential of the human race shines through the maelstrom that can engulf major choices. A strong advocate of engaged listening ("listening is more than just waiting to speak"), she urges applying the soothing balm that comes when, in timely fashion, we press the Pause button of the mind.

She is a thoughtful optimist, and it serves her readers well.

Judith Morgan
Co-author of Dr. Seuss & Mr. Geisel
(Random House, 1995)
La Jolla, CA
January 2013

INTRODUCTION

A rancher, when asked about his philosophy of fence building, said, "If you don't have time to do it right the first time, when will you have time to do it over?"

Our society worships speed and demands immediate solutions. We praise those who think and act quickly. As a result, expensive and time-consuming "do-overs" abound. Whether it's buying a luxury car on impulse, marrying or divorcing in a moment of high passion, waiting until the eleventh hour to pass critical legislation, or plunging a country into war, hasty decisions can have long-lasting and damaging consequences. Perhaps the hastiest decision of all is procrastination. Today's political landscape is strewn with the fallout from avoiding tough choices.

It's not just hot button issues like abortion, climate change, guns and health care that challenge our civility. In our personal lives as well, people and values clash. Unless we have chosen to avoid conflict altogether, we are tempted to move fast and get beyond our discomfort as quickly as possible.

Think of a tough choice as a courtyard surrounded by a multistory building. Each of us stands somewhere in that building, looking down from our unique vantage point. We see things differently. Our interests and values may not be the same.

This book shows ways to slow down in the face of tough choices and move deliberately among and through conflicting perspectives and values. Most of us prefer to avoid conflict. The irony is, of course, that sitting with and managing conflict in our daily lives is often the best way to resolve it.

Decisions are difficult because they often force us to choose, not so much between good and evil, but among competing goods. What matters most: Religious freedom or civil rights? National security or individual privacy? Sanctity of life or a woman's reproductive autonomy? Safety of other drivers or respect for an elderly parent's independence?

Good decisions can hurt. Not because we could have done better, not because we have made a bad decision, but because even the best decisions can have downsides. Tough choices frequently force us to compromise values that matter. Even the strongest decisions can bring regret.

This book shows how you, your families, neighbors and others can come together to make strong personal decisions, especially when perspectives and values collide. At the end of the book are two blank worksheets for you to use as you work through tough choices. Feel free to copy, use and share with others.

Mediators remind us, "Go slow to go fast." Pause. Take a breath.

Let's begin.

SEEING
Where am I?
Where are you?
What matters?

BELIEVING

DOING

*The foolish reject what they see,
not what they think; the wise reject what they
think, not what they see.*

—Huang Po

WHERE AM I?

We see the world, not the way it is,
but the way we are.
—Talmud

Road Hazard

Charlotte's father had taught her to drive when she was 15. More than 70 years later, at a sprightly age 85, she still remembered his advice. "Assume everyone else on the road is crazy." She hadn't had an accident, ever, until yesterday, when she had run a stop sign in her own rural neighborhood. Fortunately, no one in the other car or hers suffered anything more than bruises and sore muscles. "You know how much Mae and Lorene like to talk. I think I got distracted." She was always nagging her aged neighbors, whom she frequently drove for shopping and appointments, to buckle up and stop bickering in the back seat.

Charlotte's only child, Jeff, lived 50 miles away, and he and his wife had talked in recent months about Charlotte's driving. They were increasingly worried. "You know how much Mom's driving means to her and all her friends she drives for errands, doctors' appointments, not to mention bingo with Mae and Lorene. I asked her just last week what she'd do when she could no longer drive. She said, 'Well, you know that's a long time off. Maybe by then they'll have some transportation for us old folks. But we don't have to worry about that now, do we!'"

Jeff talked to Charlotte's doctor last night after the accident and expressed concern about his mother's driving. Dr. Barton, no spring chicken himself, assured Jeff and his wife, "Charlotte's just fine. She and I both think she's a good driver. She promised me she'd stay off the Interstate, except when she takes her friend for radiation therapy in the next county. I don't know what she'd do without Charlotte. She really holds this farming community together. We're lucky to have her."

Perspective

Background and experience create our perspective.
We all bring one.
First, know yourself.

Where to start? A good place to begin, actually the only place, is where you are standing right now. Assume you are Jeff, Charlotte's son. What is your first reaction? Maybe it's, "I knew this day would come. I wish Dr. Barton would take the lead here. We're talking about safety." Of course, were you to ask Charlotte, or Dr. Barton, or Mae and Lorene about their first reaction, you might hear something else:

> *I am careful, I stay off the freeway whenever possible, and honestly, I don't know what I'd do if I couldn't drive.*

> *Charlotte and I have talked about her driving. It's so important for her independence, and she really is careful where she drives. Many of my patients depend on her.*

If it weren't for Charlotte, we wouldn't have any way of getting to appointments or activities. Public transportation in our rural area just doesn't exist. She's a godsend.

What to Do

Again, think of a difficult decision as a courtyard where each person's angle of vision is unique. It may be similar to someone standing nearby, but very different from those looking down from the opposite side of the building. Only you can occupy your space. No one can see things exactly as you do. Perspective is neither good nor bad. It just is. Before you make a final decision, you need to know where you're standing, and why you see the issue as you do.

▸ Ask yourself, what's my first reaction?

▸ Think about where this reaction comes from.

From one's **role**?	*It's hard when it's your mother.*
	I'm her physician.
	My friends rely on me.
From **experience**?	*I've already been through this with my father.*
	My medical practice is mainly geriatric, and I confront this issue several times a day.
	I live alone. There is no one else to drive me and my friends.
From one's **place** in the family or community?	*How do you tell your mother she can't drive anymore?*
	In our culture and community, being able to drive is essential to remaining independent.
	The day I can't drive is the day I die.

▶ Clarify what's at stake.

> Safety
> Independence
> Basic activities of daily living
> Anything else?

Why Perspective Matters

We can't even think about an issue without first framing it. Perspective colors how we see, what we notice and what we can't see. But we aren't stuck with our first reaction. We can change perspective. How? By noticing our first reaction and then asking others to describe theirs. How we pose a question determines our answer. We want to get it right.

A problem properly stated is half solved.
—John Dewey

WHERE ARE YOU?

> *Isolation is the worst possible counselor.*
> —Miguel de Unamuno

Not in My Backyard

Sally and Tom lived in their suburban neighborhood for over 20 years. They raised their family there, sent their children to the local schools, and saw the neighborhood change over time as immigrants moved in and many of their original neighbors left. Sally and Tom made the decision to remain. They truly enjoyed living in a community with such ethnic and financial diversity. They made a conscious effort to welcome newcomers and attend neighborhood association meetings, where Tom was recently elected president.

At his second meeting as president, his next-door neighbor Steve, a relative newcomer, but someone who immediately took an active interest in the neighborhood, spoke up:

> *Tom, we've just learned that there are plans to build an Islamic center nearby. They are going to ask for the association's blessing to build. They point out that there are other churches in our neighborhood, and there is a small but growing Muslim popu-*

lation here who want to worship closer to home. They've even suggested we visit a mosque in another neighborhood to see how they did it.

I have spoken to a number of our neighbors, and we all agree. No way. I have collected signatures from about 40 percent of our association membership, all opposing the center. We would like you, as our president, to spearhead our drive to keep the Islamic center from being built here.

Dialogue

**Listening is more than just waiting to speak.
Discover what others see that you don't.
You might be changed by what others say.**

Tom was clear about his own perspective: Citizens and communities thrive on tolerance and diversity. Obviously, Steve and some others did not agree. Tempted though he was to reply, "No!" to Steve's request, Tom took Sally's advice and invited Steve and some other association members to their house to talk about the petition. Tom started with, "I think many of you know that my first reaction was to say 'No' to your request. I realize, however, that I have no idea where you are coming from on this. Listening to each other is important. Tell me how you see things."

Steve looked somewhat uncomfortable, but spoke first: "I moved here from lower Manhattan, hoping to get away from the awful memories of 9/11. A good friend of mine died in one of the World Trade Center towers." Marie, Steve's other next-door neighbor, spoke next: "I've felt so sorry for Steve ever since I heard his story. I signed this petition because it seemed to mean so much to him."

Tom looked around the room, making sure everyone who wanted to speak had the opportunity to do so. Bob, a long-time resident, was the last to speak: "I don't know any Muslims. I'm not sure I want my children going to school with them, especially if they wear head scarves and pray in public."

What to Do

Remember the courtyard image in the first chapter? Each signer of the petition is standing somewhere in that building, looking down on the Islamic center issue. Eventually, Tom must make a decision. He is clear about his own initial reaction, but he realized he had no idea where the others stood. He decided to ask, he listened, and others spoke their mind. He learned, for the first time, why Steve had moved to their neighborhood. He was moved by Marie's friendship for Steve. And he heard genuine concern in Bob's voice.

> **Ask open, inviting questions.**

Steve, tell me what's on your mind here.

> **Don't interrupt.**

It's tempting, when someone else is talking, especially if we disagree with them, to challenge them, or at least prepare our rebuttal while they're talking. Resist that temptation and really listen to what they're saying.

> **Ask for clarification; reflect back.**

One way to make sure you've listened is to repeat aloud what you've heard, without judging.

Steve, those memories must still haunt you. Clearly, a safe neighborhood really matters to you.

Marie, Steve is fortunate to have such a good friend.

Bob, I too fear what's foreign or strange to me.

Why Dialogue Matters

Conversations about heated issues often take the form of serial monologues. You talk from your script, I from mine, and rarely if ever do we open ourselves to those who have different or opposing perspectives. If we do listen, it's usually to rebut or critique. Honoring differences keeps the climate respectful, provides valuable insight into why others hold the views they do, and increases the odds of creating a decision with more, not less, buy-in from those affected. Skilled decision makers make stronger and clearer decisions when they've listened to and involved those who have a stake in the decision, especially those with whom they disagree. Dialogue matters.

We have two ears and a mouth so that we can listen twice as much as we speak.
—Epictetus

WHAT MATTERS?

Our lives begin to end the day we become silent about things that matter.
—Martin Luther King Jr.

Coming Out

The headline scared her. "Gay college freshman commits suicide." Jenny had just been accepted to her first choice of colleges. Her parents were so proud of their only child, the first in their family to go to college. This coming weekend, following Sunday worship, their church was holding a special graduation celebration for Jenny. Although Jenny didn't always agree with the church's stand on social issues, the pastor and the church community had helped her family through some tough times. She read the title of Sunday's sermon: *The Sin of Homosexuality.* This past year Jenny realized she was a lesbian. She had thought she would be better off leaving for college without telling her parents. After reading the headline, she wasn't so sure.

Values

Notice what matters.
Go deeper; go slower.
Keep values language simple.

Decisions reveal what matters to us, what we value. Sometimes we don't know, even for ourselves, how many different values are in play until we slow down and think about it. Jenny knew she had to be true to herself. She also wanted to protect her parents from information she feared would distress them, and to respect the church community that had done so much for her and her parents. She also admitted, to herself, she was scared: scared to tell her parents, scared what might happen if she didn't. All this mattered to her. All these were values important to her.

What to Do

The word "values" is loaded. Often talk about values leads to dead ends: too much heat, not enough light, rarely common ground. Sometimes values talk stays at such an abstract level that, while few are offended, no concrete guidance comes from it. "Be true to yourself. Respect your parents. Do no harm."

Like the tip of an iceberg, values words are code for powerful and personal interests and beliefs that lie beneath the surface. The solution is to go deeper. To bring values to life, ask yourself, "What does 'Be true to yourself,' or 'Respect your elders,' mean in this situation? Why are these values important?" Answer in everyday, simple language. Here are some steps you can take to build your values list.

- Identify the stakeholders.

    Who's looking down onto the courtyard? Who has a real stake in the decision? Jenny, of course. Also, her parents and the church community.

- Ask what matters to them.

    Because each of them comes to this issue from their own perspective, their roles, background and experience, and what matters to them will likely differ. While we might imagine what matters to them, asking them directly is best.

- Encourage stories.

    We humans are hardwired to be storytellers. We tell stories to find direction, make sense of a situation, and get our bearings. Jenny, her parents and the people in their church all have stories that explain their values more completely. Resist the temptation to tell someone else's story for them. Inviting others' stories, through dialogue, inevitably softens the conflict among values.

Why Values Matter

Most values talk is like an oil slick that remains on the surface of the water: It shimmers but shares little chemistry with what lies beneath. Superficial values talk can also be toxic to the deeper meanings beneath the surface. Values come to life only when we place them in our current situation.

Sometimes we are blind even to our own values, what they are and why they matter so much to us. Often we have no clue what really matters to others and why, although we are quick to assume we know. These unspoken realities and misperceptions are the elephant in the room. We dislodge the elephant only through listening and speaking about what really matters to everyone involved, and why.

> *It is not hard to make decisions*
> *when you know what your values are.*
> —Roy Disney

SEEING

BELIEVING What matters most?
Why?
Must it hurt?

DOING

*Nothing is as easy as deceiving yourself,
for what you wish you readily believe.*
—Demosthenes

WHAT MATTERS MOST?

the black spaces:
as much star
as star!
—Anita Virgil

Home

Emily and Ned had talked about the future, until Ned's advanced Alzheimer's had finally made serious discussion impossible. Several times Ned had asked Emily, "Will you promise me you won't spend our savings on care I won't even know I am getting?" Emily had avoided making any promises, but, after 49 years of marriage, she knew what he meant, and his wishes mattered to her more than anything else. So did his well-being. She had told Ned, "I promise to do whatever I can to keep you comfortable and peaceful." He had simply said, "Thank you. But don't forget to take care of yourself."

The problem now was, the only place where Ned was peaceful was at home. Emily had tried several facilities: nice places that cost less than half as much as around-the-clock in-home care. But Ned required heavy sedation to control his extreme agitation, except when he was home. They had the funds to pay for caregivers to assist Emily. She couldn't handle it otherwise. But there wouldn't be much left for her by the time Ned died, probably within the next year or two. By now Emily was the only one Ned recognized, if only intermittently, although when he did he would always greet her with, "How's the light of my life?"

Good vs. Good

Go beyond right vs. wrong.
Identify competing goods.
Find your guiding star.

A common misconception is that decisions are tough because we must determine right from wrong. Not so. Granted, avoiding doing what's wrong is the first, essential step. But the next, much harder step requires both choosing and forsaking values that really matter to us, because we can't honor them all in a single decision.

Emily wanted to respect Ned's clear wishes. She had promised she would do whatever it took to keep him comfortable and peaceful. And she certainly needed to look out for her own well-being while Ned was still alive and afterwards. The more she thought about it, the more she realized she had to prioritize among several values that were truly important, yet in conflict. She had to find out what was most important. She had to find her guiding star.

What to Do

In our public and professional lives, ethics talk focuses almost exclusively on what people may have done wrong. While this is important, it ignores values-based decision making's unique contribution:

identifying positive values and what's important; committing to what's most important; then acting based on these top values.

- **List what would be wrong to do, then list the positive values. What would you like to achieve?**

    Of course Emily would not consider anything except the highest quality care for Ned. Nor would she admit him to a facility and then essentially abandon him to get on with her life. Still, she was left with a real conflict among important values: honoring Ned's wish not to spend money on care he wouldn't notice; keeping her promise to do whatever it took to keep him peaceful; looking out for herself, psychologically and financially.

- **Let your mind's eye adjust to what's most important.**

    Emily spent some time thinking about all those values that mattered to her, and why.

- **Find the value that shines brightest.**

    While she could make a good case for each of the values, she kept coming back to what seemed most important to her: doing everything she could to keep Ned comfortable. The other values mattered. This one mattered most.

Why Competing Goods Matter

When you first step out at night and look at the sky, you might be overwhelmed by how many bright stars and beautiful constellations you see. Chances are you won't be able to spot the North Star or your favorite constellation right away. You have to let your eyes adjust. You have to orient yourself. So it is with decision making. Your emotions shift, your mind adjusts, and eventually the value that shines steadiest and brightest begins to show itself. Sit for a while with all those things that matter. Which value keeps rising to the top? That's your guiding star.

> *I don't know what the key to success is,*
> *but the key to failure is trying to please everyone.*
> —Bill Cosby

WHY?

A great many people think they are thinking when they are merely rearranging their prejudices.
—William James

Faith and Family

Bob and Anita met in college while working on the reelection campaign for their state's Democratic U.S. senator. They called themselves progressive liberals and had remained politically active after marriage and as they raised their daughter, Wendy. Wendy did not share their political activism, and she found herself drawn to a local, fundamentalist evangelical church, which she joined as a freshman in high school. Although they did not attend church, Bob and Anita told Wendy they supported her in her personal journey of faith, even though they strongly disagreed with some of the church's social and political teachings.

Wendy was an excellent student, always held part-time jobs in high school, and contributed to the college savings account her parents had started when she was born. Bob and Anita realized that, even with the savings account, college expenses were going to strain their budget, but they were willing to make that sacrifice.

Wendy indicated that she wanted to apply for early admission, since there was only one college she wanted to attend: a fully accredited, private, out-of-state evangelical Christian college sponsored by her church. While scholarships, loans and work-study could defray some of the costs, Bob and Anita were still looking at a likely annual outlay of at least $30,000. And, they admitted to each other, they were concerned about the unabashed fundamentalist influence on the curriculum.

Accountability

Values have deep, personal meanings.
Know why your top value is your top value.
Effective decisions grow from deeply understood values.

Since their college days, Anita and Bob had committed themselves to issues of social justice, civil rights and diversity. While their parents hadn't always agreed with their positions or their "incessant protesting," as Bob's father had complained, both families valued independent thinking. Anita and Bob promised each other that they too would encourage their children to think for themselves. Clearly, Wendy was challenging them. Many of her church's teachings on social issues were at odds with her parents' values. Education was likewise important to them. After all, it went hand in hand with thinking for oneself. While their finances were modest, they had agreed early on they would make every effort to provide a college education for their daughter.

What to Do

It's one thing to know what your top value is. It's another to know why. Understanding the reasons why you picked, say, fostering independent thinking in your children, strengthens your commitment to that value, especially in the face of other important but competing values. Such understanding also helps you explain and justify your top value to those who may disagree. They may or may not be persuaded, but they will understand your position.

- **Understand why your top value is so meaningful.**

    As Bob and Anita talked about those values that were most important to them, including civil rights, respecting difference, and lifting up those less fortunate than themselves, they realized that the values all flowed from a deep commitment to the worth of individuals as self-determining persons. They wondered, how could they deny that for their daughter?

- **Advocate for what you deem most important, especially with those who disagree with you. Ask them to do the same with their top value.**

    Bob and Anita certainly experienced some pushback from their friends and colleagues who shared their political and social values. Their immediate reactions were, 'How can you compromise such important values?' However, when Bob and Anita explained to them how deep their commitment was to individual self-determination, their opposition softened.

- **Commit to your guiding star.**

    Settling on our top value does not mean, however, that the other values are no longer important to us. Relegating them to a lower priority can cause us some regret. We have to compromise other values that matter. We have to leave them behind. A good decision includes the price paid.

Why Accountability Matters

Difficult choices test us. They may cost us something. Nevertheless, once we have figured out what matters most and why, we should lean into our top value rather than shy away from something we don't like.

> *I leave this rule for others when I'm dead.*
> *Be always sure you're right, then go ahead.*
> —David Crockett

MUST IT HURT?

> *A weak man has doubts before a decision,*
> *a strong man has them afterwards.*
> —Karl Kraus

Privilege

Jeremy and Lou had been friends since elementary school. Even though Jeremy's family had moved to the suburbs and sent him to a private high school while Lou attended public school, the two of them still saw each other nearly every weekend. Jeremy had just been accepted to an out-of-state university. Lou's parents expected him to go to work in the family restaurant after high school. Lou's family was struggling in the recession and his father had told him: "We need you at the restaurant. College will have to wait."

One night, at a party at a friend's house, police responded to a neighbor's call and arrested Jeremy, Lou and others for possession of marijuana and cocaine, and for underage drinking. Jeremy insisted to his father that he and Lou had each just smoked pot, and very little of that. "I know it was dumb. You know Lou and I don't go in for that sort of thing. We're both really sorry."

His father was furious but said he would ask his golfing friend, a lawyer, to get the charges against Jeremy dropped. "I know people who can get this done." When Jeremy asked about helping Lou, his father replied, "Lou is on his own. Maybe his family can find someone. You've got to look out for yourself."

Downsides

Most difficult decisions have them.
Some values will be compromised.
Some people will be hurt.

Jeremy was torn between conflicting values: his long-standing friendship with Lou; his relationship with his father; his future, both at college and after. As he reviewed what was most important to him, he kept coming back to friendship and his loyalty to Lou as his top value. "Without friendship, what is there? Friends don't abandon each other. If I walk away from Lou, simply because I have resources that he doesn't, I betray what is most important to me." Jeremy also knew he was risking his father's wrath, not to mention the impact of a drug conviction going forward.

What to Do

Each of the cases presented in this book has had obvious downsides. Decision makers have had to compromise, even violate, values that matter deeply to them and to others. The most challenging decisions are not about right vs. wrong or good vs. bad. Instead, they are choices between right and right.

Few, if any, important decisions benefit everyone and burden no one, including the decision maker. Good decisions are forged from competing goods. Regret is part of the price paid for our thorough analysis and careful attention. When we understand who is involved and what matters to them, we appreciate why some will be disappointed, hurt or angry.

- **Identify the downsides.**

    If Jeremy chooses not to "go it alone," he risks alienating his father, and perhaps jeopardizing his college and subsequent professional career. If he follows his father's advice, he abandons Lou and sacrifices his most important friendship.

- **Admit those values you most regret compromising.**

    Jeremy was clear about this. Compromising his friendship with Lou would bring him the most regret.

- **Be honest about who stands to lose.**

    No matter what Jeremy chooses, he will compromise important values and hurt others. If he follows his father's advice, he will hurt Lou, Lou's family and probably even himself, given how important Lou's friendship is to him. If Jeremy chooses to support Lou, his father and his family will undoubtedly suffer, as will he, insofar as his future depends on an unblemished record.

Why Downsides Matter

Framing conflicts only as a struggle between good and evil underestimates their moral complexity. The difficult moral struggle lies in choosing between mutually exclusive, fundamental values, without then turning against those values left behind. Commitment and choice are rarely innocent. They are not harm free. Tough decisions can hurt.

> *Courage is the first among human qualities because it is the one on which all others depend.*
> —Aristotle

SEEING

BELIEVING

DOING
What are my choices?
What fits?
What do I say?

a white lotus —
the monk decides
to cut it!

—Yosa Buson

WHAT ARE MY CHOICES?

> *Two roads diverged in a wood, and I—*
> *I took the one less traveled by,*
> *And that has made all the difference.*
> —Robert Frost

Jeff, Tom and Jenny Consider Their Options

As Jeff thought about how to confront his mother, Charlotte, about her driving, he realized that, first and foremost, he was Charlotte's son.

Before he left for the next neighborhood association meeting to discuss the contentious Islamic center issue, Tom told his wife that he had decided to focus on his role as president of the neighborhood association.

Jenny, after talking with her best friend about whether to "come out" to her parents about being gay, realized that her first responsibility was to her own identity and personal integrity.

While each of these decision makers was clear about where they stood and which perspective and role should prevail, settling on what was most important in a sea of conflicting values was more difficult. Eventually, each committed to what mattered most.

For Jeff, it was respect for his mother, and her safety as well as others'.

For Tom, it was living his commitment to diversity: listening to different voices and making room at the table for all positions, especially those he found offensive.

For Jenny, it was remaining true to herself while respecting her parents in the process.

What should they do next? What are their options?

Choosing vs. Deciding

Tough choices pose different options.

Each option has foreseeable consequences.

Decisions are strongest when they flow from your top value.

"Decide" comes from the Latin word *decaedere*, which means "to cut off." Difficult decisions often leave us with the feeling that we have simply settled for the last option standing. When we go with the least worse option, we may hold our nose and say, "Okay. Whatever."

There is a better way. The dynamic of affirming our guiding values and using them to prioritize our options, rather than aggressively chopping off what we don't like, connects us in a positive way to our decisions and contributes to their effectiveness and staying power. We have made a choice.

What to Do

▶ Review your options.

At dinner Jeff told his wife:

> I am pretty clear about what's most important to me. Now I have to choose among what I see as my three options:
>
> Do nothing and let my mother continue driving until something else happens.
>
> Make an appointment with Dr. Barton and see if I can persuade him to talk with my mother and perhaps monitor her more closely than he's done so far. She listens to him.
>
> Sit down with my mother, come clean about my serious concerns about her driving, and see what we might be able to work out.

Tom told his wife, as he was preparing his presentation to the neighborhood association:

> These seem to be my options:
>
> Agree to Steve's request and oppose building the Islamic center.
>
> Formally oppose Steve's request at the next meeting and urge support for building the center.
>
> Visit the neighboring mosque, and see how it works in their neighborhood.
>
> Resign, or wait until I am voted out.

Jenny described her thoughts to her best friend:

> As I see it, these are my three choices. What do you think?
>
> Don't say anything to my parents or the pastor.

Speak privately with the pastor before next Sunday's service.

Speak to my parents tonight.

- **Don't settle for the least worse option.**

  Jeff admitted the easy way out would be to let his mother keep driving. Tom thought seriously about resigning and handing the Islamic center issue over to someone else. A part of Jenny just wanted to preserve family harmony, not say anything and leave for college with her secret intact.

- **Commit to your top value.**

  Despite the temptation to "cut and run," Jeff, Tom and Jenny had already clarified what mattered most and listed their options. Their next step would be to commit to their top values and select that option that aligned best with their guiding stars.

Why Choosing Matters

The temptation to rush to a decision is powerful. Remaining patient this close to making a decision is hard, especially when you may already have a preferred decision. Ask yourself, "Have I considered all my realistic options?" Check with a trusted friend or advisor. "Am I missing other alternatives?" Working from an expanded set of options ensures you've not missed something important, something that others might have thought of. When you focus on your top value, you find yourself leaning into the strongest option. You choose.

Our actions are the ground on which we stand.
—Gautama Buddha

WHAT FITS?

> *[The] highest duty and the highest proof*
> *of wisdom—that deed and word*
> *should be in accord...*
> —Seneca the Younger

Emily, Bob and Anita, and Jeremy Decide

Emily found herself faced with a stark choice. She could spend down their savings on home care, or she could put Ned in an Alzheimer's facility at half the cost.

Bob and Anita had not expected to be faced with choosing whether to remain true to their values of openness and inclusion or financially supporting their daughter's choice to attend an evangelical college that seemed to oppose such values.

Jeremy couldn't remember ever having to cross his father in such a serious way. Should he follow his father's instructions to look out for himself, or should he put his friendship for Lou ahead of his own immediate, perhaps even long-term, gain?

Alignment

Decisions aligned with values build integrity.
"Outlier" options can exert a strong pull.
More downsides may appear once you make a decision.

By now you have probably imagined what you'd do in these situations. Perhaps you decided as soon as you read the case. You can't always avoid jumping to a decision. You can, however, pause and temporarily "park" your first decision, while you reflect on yours and others' points of view and values. If you're the decision maker, take the time to find your top value, your guiding star. Go slow to get it right. Getting it right means making a decision that flows directly from what matters most to you. Sometimes the flow is smooth and obvious. Sometimes your top value leads you to a decision that hurts. Sometimes that first reaction still calls you but clearly conflicts with your top value. Alignment of value and action is the heart of decisions that last.

What to Do

▸ **Test each option against your guiding value.**

Emily had struggled long enough with her decision. She was clear that what was most important to her was keeping Ned comfortable. She had tried a top Alzheimer's facility for what she thought was a sufficient period of time, but Ned remained agitated and clearly uncomfortable unless heavily sedated. Yes, her savings were being depleted. There was no good face to put on that. But it was most important to her that she maximize Ned's quality of life while he was able to experience it. Home was where that happened.

- **Consider the consequences of each option.**

  Bob and Anita were still struggling. Their commitment to social values, such as full legal and social rights for gays and lesbians, women's reproductive autonomy, and separation of church and state in all matters governmental and public, went to the core of their value system. It was how they treated each other, their family, their friends and their community. Wendy's church, and the curriculum of her college of choice, seemed to fly in the face of these values.

  Also important was their commitment to their daughter's right of self-determination, a value, they came to realize, that was the basis of their social principles. People have a right to be who they are, to make their own choices, to believe what they will. Self-determination was, perhaps, the value common to all their principles. While it bothered them that a consequence of supporting their daughter in her college choice might undermine someone else's self-determination, it was a contradiction, an unintended but certainly foreseeable consequence, they decided to live with. Fidelity to the principle of self-determination for Wendy clearly pointed to their supporting her in her decision. And so they did, but not without real concern.

- **Don't be surprised if there is an option that appeals but doesn't align with your top value. Where does that lead you?**

  For Jeremy, what mattered most to him was clear. He wanted Lou, his best friend, to have access to the same legal resources he had. His first thought was to confront his father and say, "If you don't help Lou, then I'm not accepting your lawyer friend's help. We either float or sink together. That's what friends do." But he knew to do so would incur his father's wrath. Simply put, he was afraid of his father. He also feared for his future. Knowing what mattered most to him, loyalty to his friend, didn't allay these fears. He couldn't shake the temptation to accept the lawyer's help. For the first time in their friendship, Jeremy couldn't bring himself to be honest with Lou. It was a secret he just couldn't share. And so he prepared to tell his father to go ahead and hire him a lawyer.

Why Alignment Matters

Decisions work best, they last, and others go along or at least are less likely to oppose them, when there is clear alignment between the decisions and the values behind them. Decision makers who have thought about what is most important to them, and why, and who explain this to those affected by the decision, earn credibility in a way that spin can never achieve. Spin weaves a story around a decision that panders to what listeners may want to hear, but conceals the real agenda or values driving the decision. Decisions cloaked in spin wither and die. So does the decision maker's credibility.

A man's character is formed by his decisions.
—Jean-Paul Sartre

WHAT DO I SAY?

> *Sometimes, to be silent is to lie.*
> —Miguel de Unamuno

Jeff, Tom and Jenny Explain

Jeff

Over dinner, Jeff talked with his wife about his thoughts so far:

> It's clear that I am approaching this as my mother's son. I also know that the others who are involved—my mother, Dr. Barton, Mom's friends, and, I suppose, other drivers who would have something to say if they were asked—may see things differently. Their values are important, but this is my decision.
>
> I need to be clear about what matters to me. Safety (my mother's and other drivers'), Mom's independence and support for her friends who count on her to take them places are all important values, but I can't honor them all at the same time. As I think about values, I keep coming back to these: I want to do what is most respectful of my mother, and I want to keep her and others out of harm's way.

Together, Jeff and his wife tested each option against Jeff's top values. Option one, do nothing, clearly conflicted with the value of safety, and it didn't really address the value of respectfulness. It mostly avoided the issue.

Option two, visit Dr. Barton, if it led to Charlotte's not driving any more, might address the safety value, but it seemed to Jeff that he would not be respecting his mother if he went behind her back.

This left option three, talk with his mother. While the safety consequences could go either way, it clearly was the most respectful decision Jeff could imagine.

Tom

Tom asked his wife to listen to his decision-making process:

> *While it's hard for me to put aside my strong commitment to diversity, even temporarily, I'm the neighborhood association president, and I need to represent the entire neighborhood. I learned a great deal from Steve, Marie and Bob about what matters to them: safety, being neighborly, fear of the 'other.' And I think they learned something as well. I want to build on that.*
>
> *I am clear that tolerance and respect for others is my top value. That applies not only to those advocating for building an Islamic center, but also to those who oppose it. So any decision to cut off dialogue, whether to give immediate approval or to deny the request, would violate my value of understanding and accepting others. That leaves me with the third option, accept the invitation from the Islamic center across town that went through a similar process with a skeptical community. I have asked Steve, Marie and Bob to come with me, and to bring anyone else who would like to attend.*

Jenny

Jenny was fortunate to have a good friend to listen to her while she went through her decision-making process. It did not take her long to realize that figuring out how to honor her own identity was what triggered this journey in the first place. Still, she appreciated that her parents' cultural and religious values, and certainly those of the pastor and other church members, would likely conflict with hers. In the end, however, it was being faithful to who she was that shone brightest among the other important values. Personal integrity demanded nothing less.

She and her friend had agreed that there were several ways she could proceed. She could say nothing to her parents or the pastor, sit through Sunday's sermon, and eventually leave for college without having said anything. She could approach the pastor privately before next Sunday, talk with him and, perhaps, ask him for advice or at least to reconsider the content of his sermon. Or she could speak to her parents before next Sunday's worship service. Whether they then spoke to the pastor would be up to her parents.

Jenny decided that her top value, honoring her own identity and sense of personal integrity, led her to talk with her parents as soon as possible. But she was scared. She feared they would be angry, hurt, disappointed. What if they disowned her or insisted she get treatment to "cure" her homosexuality? Still, her friend reminded her, she had come this far.

Communication

Honest explanations improve a decision's success and strength.
Explain your decision to those affected.
Be candid about your decision's downsides.

Making a decision and failing to communicate it is like being in a room with the windows closed and the curtains drawn, expecting people outside to know what you are doing. Most decisions, even when made in private, need support from those affected. For decisions to succeed, those who make them must explain them honestly and thoroughly.

What to Do

▷ **Communicate with clarity, honesty and respect.**

Listen to Jeff, Tom and Jenny as they complete their decision making process. As you add their earlier thoughts to these closing explanations, check how clearly they have communicated:

their own perspective
how others might see things differently
what values are important to them and to others
what is their guiding star
an explanation of their top value
a list of options and possible consequences of each
clear alignment between top value and decision
honesty about the decision's downside

Jeff

Jeff went to visit his mother the next day. "Mom, this is really difficult for me. You remember the time we had with Dad as his dementia progressed, and we finally took his keys away from him. I don't know whether we handled that situation as well as we might have, but we were scared, weren't we. So I really want to do this well. As far as I can tell, you're still a good driver, but last week's accident might be a good wakeup call for us. I know how much your friends depend on you. And it seems that Dr. Barton doesn't have any concerns. But I have some real concerns and want to make sure we keep an eye on things. What do you think?"

Charlotte was quiet for some time. "I know I was a bit abrupt with you right after the accident. I was terrified you were going to take away my keys like we did with your father. But I have been thinking about it since then. I love to drive and my friends really need me. But I could never forgive myself if I caused an accident where someone was seriously injured, or worse. I had asked Dr. Barton about this a couple of months ago, but he dismissed it as an unnecessary worry. I think he might be a bit concerned about his own age and driving ability. So I called my insurance company, and they told me there is a course for older drivers that, if I pass, might lower my rates. They also told me that someone could take me for a test drive to see how I do. We could set up regular drives, if that makes sense. I'm thinking of signing up for that. In the meantime, I've told Mae and Lorene that we all need to begin to think of other transportation options, for when the time comes."

Tom

Tom and a handful of his association members visited the neighboring Islamic center the following week. Steve was surprised to see a fellow research scientist with whom he worked, and who introduced himself as the president of the center. Members of the Islamic center had prepared food and invited non-Muslim community members to talk about their initial concerns and fears. By the end of the evening, even Bob had relaxed. Tom sensed that they had made progress, but that pushing for a decision was premature. In fact, his values of tolerance and respect seemed to flourish as the open-ended dialogue grew. He began to reframe the initial question from "What should I decide?" to "How can I help our communities understand each other better?"

Restating the question in this way made the next step clear. Invite members of the existing Islamic center, perhaps members of other non-Muslim faith communities, and the Muslims wanting to build a center in Tom's neighborhood, to a special neighborhood association meeting. "Let's invite leaders from other neighborhood churches as well," Tom said. "We could have a potluck." Steve, Marie and Bob agreed. Tom sensed they were relieved that the pressure of making an immediate decision was lessened. He knew he was.

Jenny

That evening after dinner, Jenny came into the living room and told her parents she needed to talk with them.

"Mom, Dad, this is really hard and I'm scared. But I need to be honest with you. I thought about not telling you and just going to college with my own secret. You're my family and I want you to know. I need your help. I'm a lesbian. I think I have known this for a long time. Now it's really clear. And I don't think I can sit through this Sunday's worship service and listen to a sermon on 'The Sin of Homosexuality.'"

Jenny's mother started to cry. Her father was silent. They sat there for what seemed to Jenny an eternity.

Finally her mother spoke. "Oh, Jenny, we just haven't known what to do. This really isn't a surprise, but we kept hoping it wasn't so. We thought about asking the pastor, but we were afraid of what he would say. I have a friend at work whose son is gay. I've never brought it up with her. I was embarrassed for her, but maybe she can help me understand how to get through this. Maybe you would go with me when I talk with her? I just don't know what we'll tell the pastor."

Jenny said, "Of course I'll go, Mom. Dad, what about you?"

Jenny's father waited for a while. Finally he said, "You know we love you, but I just don't know what to think. It seems so wrong. This will take time. It must have been hard for you to tell us. I think your mother and I should go to church this Sunday, but you don't have to. Just come to the party afterwards, like you've done in the past. Your mother and I will talk more about this. We'll figure out what to say to the pastor."

Why Communication Matters

Decisions poorly communicated, or not communicated at all, routinely fail. Unexplained decisions resemble the tip of an iceberg. Most of their body remains hidden to the surface observer, encouraging the avid conspiracy theorist to assume the worst. The antidote is simple, though not always easy: be transparent. Let in the sunshine.

> *Wisdom is the reward you get for a lifetime of listening when you'd have preferred to talk.*
> —Doug Larson

FINAL THOUGHTS

CONCLUSION

Tough choices get our juices flowing. We confront them, in our families, our neighborhoods, our places of work. When we do so, and don't deny or avoid them, it is the pace and quality of our decision-making process that will determine the strength of our decision.

Tough choices present different kinds of conflict. Sometimes it's people who see the issue in altogether different ways. Sometimes it's values and interests that collide, even within the same person. Sometimes it's competing options, each of which exerts its own pull.

Managing conflict does not banish all discomfort. Leaning into one value may force us to pivot away from something else that matters. When we commit to one approach we may turn our back on other perspectives. Strong decisions have downsides, but weak ones have more. Effective decision makers cop to their regrets.

What is the payoff? When we consider different perspectives we enlarge our angle of vision. When we involve others we build invaluable support, even among those who might disagree with us. When we take time to see the different values and interests at play, we are less likely to overlook something that really matters to us or to others. When we lead with our top value and use it, our decision has a force and staying power not otherwise possible. When we communicate openly and honestly to those affected, we won't, through our silence, squander an otherwise strong, good decision.

Tough choices will never be easy, and others will continue to disagree with us. The deeper we dig, the more competing good options we are likely to unearth. Nevertheless, strong decisions build on themselves. Each time we bring potential adversaries to the table, it is a little easier. We become more efficient as we slow down, listen deeply and take responsibility. Strong decisions pave the way for handling future challenges. Practice won't make perfect, just better.

The world needs all the strong decisions it can get.

WORKSHEETS

DECISION-MAKING WORKSHEET

Use this worksheet to move carefully through your decision-making process. Go slow. Listen well. Don't assume.

SEEING

Where am I?
My first reaction is…

Where are you?
Others' first reactions [ask them!] are…

What matters?
Values and interests important to me and to others are…

BELIEVING

What matters most?
My top value or interest is…

Why?
I chose this as my top value or interest because…

Must it hurt?
Important values and interests I can't fully honor are…

DOING

What are my choices?
As I see it, my options are…

What fits?
The option that aligns most closely with my top value is…

What do I say?
I need to explain my decision to…

What I will tell them is…*

*Use the Decision Summary Form.

DECISION SUMMARY FORM

Once you have made your decision, identify those who have a right and a need to hear what you have decided, and why. Make sure your explanation includes the following, in whatever order you think is best.

THE DECISION

State your decision in direct, simple language.
My decision is…

THE REASONS

List and describe the values and interests you considered.
What I and others identified as important values include…

Identify your top value, among all the values and interests.
In the end, what matters most to me is…

Explain the reasons you picked this as your top value.
This value matters most to me because…

THE DOWNSIDES*

Admit what you struggled with as you reached your decision. Who will bear a burden?
Those who may not like or even suffer from my decision include…

Acknowledge those values you compromised or left behind.
The values and interests important to me, and to others, that I couldn't fully honor, include…

*While you don't have to beat yourself up about the downsides, your credibility and your decision's effectiveness demand honesty. Others clearly see the downsides. If you don't mention them, people see you either as sloppy (didn't you listen to those who disagree?) or indifferent (don't you even care about your decision's negative consequences?).

Also, resist the temptation to mitigate the downsides with vague promises, unless you are prepared to offer concrete next steps that truly will help the situation. Usually you, the decision maker, are the only one who feels better. Bake sales, blue ribbon commissions, and promises to "revisit the issue" just kick the can down the road. The predictable outcome: cynicism.

ACKNOWLEDGEMENTS

Pause has come this far through the efforts of many.

Thanks to:

Mark Bennett: colleague, long-time professional partner, fellow midwife in delivering values-based decision making;

Corin Wood: editor, field tester for difficult decisions, treasured friend;

Judith Morgan: editor, rock, a wise and beautiful woman;

Friends and family whose suggestions and edits polished this final product: Lynn Abegglen, Betsy Blakely, Mary Davis, The Gyrlz, Pam Kelly, Jill Morgan, Vardit Ravitsky, Chris and Dottie Smith, Mimi Test, Anita Virgil;

April Kopp: proofreader who sees all;

Ann Zelle: photographer, artist, who captured just the right angles;

Concept Green LLC: who gave *Pause* a home; thank you Carrie Christopher;

Jennifer Pontzer: designer, editor, who, with her family Jimmy and Henry Pontzer, bring me daily joy and laughter;

Mike and Robin Gibson: my guiding stars.

SOURCES FOR QUOTATIONS

Huang Po. Listed at Belief Net, http://www.beliefnet.com/story_13576_1.html.

Talmud. Listed at http://www.care-givers.com/pages/inspiration/morequotes.

John Dewey. Listed in www.hpstrategy.com/html/quotes.html.

Miguel de Unamuno. Cited at http://www.healthyplace.com/communities/depression/related/self_help_2asp.

Epictetus. Think Exist.com Quotations Online, http://en.thinkexist.com/quotes/epictetus/ (accessed September 13, 2005).

Martin Luther King Jr. Quoted in Jocelyn Elders, "Someone Had to Speak Up," New York Times, December 20, 1994, in "Quotionary," ed. Leonard Roy Frank (New York: Random House Reference, 2001), 788.

Roy Disney. Brainy Quote, http://www.brainyquote.com/quotes/quotes/d/ (accessed on September 13, 2005).

Demosthenes. Olynthiaca, 3.19, in "Quotionary," ed. Leonard Roy Frank (New York: Random House Reference, 2001), 763.

Anita Virgil. Reprinted with author's permission.

Bill Cosby. Think Exist.com Quotations Online, http://en.thinkexist.com/quotes/bill_cosby/ (accessed September 13, 2005).

William James. Think Exist.com Quotations Online, http://en.thinkexist.com/quotes/william_james/ (accessed September 13, 2005).

David Crockett. Think Exist.com Quotations Online, http://en.thinkexist.com/quotes/david_crockett/ (accessed September 13, 2005).

Karl Kraus. Think Exist.com Quotations Online, http://en.thinkexist.com/quotes/karl_kraus/ (accessed September 13, 2005).

Aristotle. http://www.en.wikiquote.org/wiki/Aristotle.

Buson Yosa, in "Haiku Mind." Patricia Donegan (Boston: Shambhala Publications, Inc., 2008) 134. Reprinted with author's permission.

Robert Frost. "The Road Not Taken, The Poetry of Robert Frost" (New York: Holt, Rinehart, and Winston, 1969), 105.

Gautama Buddha. Cited at http://www.gatheringin.com/love.html.

Seneca the Younger. "On Practicing What You Preach," in Moral Letters to Lucilius, 14.2, trans. Richard Gummere (1918), in "Quotionary," ed. Leonard Roy Frank (New York: Random House Reference, 2001), 930.

Jean-Paul Sartre. "Notebook for an Ethics," trans. David Pellauer (Chicago: University of Chicago, 1992).

Miguel de Unamuno. Listed at http://www.nupage.ca/news_2004/n15no04a.htm.

Doug Larson. Think Exist.com Quotations Online, http://en.thinkexist.com/quotes/doug_larson/ (accessed January 16, 2013).

ABOUT THE AUTHOR

Joan McIver Gibson, Ph.D., is a philosopher and consultant in applied ethics, bioethics and values-based decision making. She has over 30 years of teaching, training, consulting and administrative work in a variety of settings: universities, business, state and federal government, health care, community and research organizations.

She graduated from Mount Holyoke College in 1965, and in 1974 earned her doctorate in philosophy from the University of California at San Diego. She currently resides in Albuquerque, New Mexico.

In 2003 she retired as the founder and director of the University of New Mexico Health Sciences Ethics Program, and for twenty years she chaired a hospital ethics committee in Albuquerque, New Mexico. She is coauthor of *A Field Guide to Good Decisions: Values in Action* (Westport, CT: Praeger, 2006), and *Health Care Ethics Committees: The Next Generation* (Chicago: American Hospital Association, 1993). She has published numerous articles and book chapters on bioethics, applied ethics, ethics committees and values-based decision making.

Visit http://joanmgibson.com to learn more.

NOTE FROM THE DESIGNER

I work in gray.

As co-owner of Concept Green, a women-owned Certified B Corporation that focuses on sustainability communications, reporting and training, I spend a lot of time thinking about issues that are not so black and white.

Black and white is easy: the stories of superheroes and villains. In the real world, we are more likely to face competing goods. Within sustainability, discussion often centers on making decisions that balance, or at least consider, economic, environmental and social aspects. This is simpler in theory: Sustainability in practice is often quite complicated. It forces us to consider deeply these competing goods as well as the downsides, the hidden and not-so-hidden costs of our decisions and actions. (In simple terms, think jobs versus environmental protection.) This complexity leads to opportunities. Putting sustainability principles into practice draws out the best in us.

My business partner, Carrie, and I took on this project partly based on our personal relationship with the author. But just as important was the book itself and the valuable guidance Joan brings, her wisdom in helping us navigate the shades of gray that tough choices present. She shows us that making good decisions is a process as well as a skill that can be honed with patience and practice.

We all work in gray.

It has been an honor to contribute design and editing to support the development and production of this book because good decisions, whether at home, at work or within our communities, have real power. Where we are today and where we will be generations from now rest on decisions.

Here's to deciding our way to a better world.

Jennifer Pontzer
Co-owner
Concept Green LLC
conceptgreen.net

A final note because I rarely get the opportunity to do this on my other projects: special thanks and tremendous love to Jimmy and Henry—the two best decisions of my life.

Made in the USA
Charleston, SC
07 May 2013